What are ...?
CAVES

Claire Llewellyn

Heinemann
LIBRARY

www.heinemann.co.uk
Visit our website to find out more information about Heinemann Library books.

To order:
 Phone 44 (0) 1865 888066
Send a fax to 44 (0) 1865 314091
Visit the Heinemann Bookshop at www.heinemann.co.uk to browse our catalogue and order online.

First published in Great Britain by Heinemann Library,
Halley Court, Jordan Hill, Oxford OX2 8EJ,
a division of Reed Educational and Professional Publishing Ltd.
Heinemann is a registered trademark of Reed Educational and Professional Publishing Ltd.

OXFORD MELBOURNE AUCKLAND
JOHANNESBURG BLANTYRE GABORONE
IBADAN PORTSMOUTH (NH) USA CHICAGO

Designed by David Oakley
Illustrated by Hardlines and Jo Brooker
Originated by Dot Gradations
Printed by South China Printing in Hong Kong/China

ISBN 0 431 02440 5 (hardback)   ISBN 0 431 02445 6 (paperback)
05 04 03 02 01   05 04 03 02 01
10 9 8 7 6 5 4 3 2 1   10 9 8 7 6 5 4 3 2 1

British Library Cataloguing in Publication Data

Llewellyn, Claire
    What are caves?. – (Take-off!)
    1.Caves – Juvenile literature
    I.Title II.Caves
    551.4'47

Acknowledgements
The publishers would like to thank the following for permission to reproduce photographs: Bruce Coleman: p.29; Ecoscene: Rob Nichol p.9, Sally Morgan p.12; FLPA: John Bastable p.8, W Wisniewski p.10, Terry Whittaker p.11, Chris Demetriou p.17; NRSC/Airphoto Group: Forestry Commission p.22, p.24; Oxford Scientific Films: Alastair Shay p.4, Kim Westerskov p.6, Martyn Chillmaid p.7, Mills Tandy p.14, JAL Cooke p.19, T Middleton p.20; Robert Harding Picture Library: AC Waltham p.15, MPH p.16, Richard Ashworth p.28; Still Pictures: D Escartin p.18; Telegraph Colour Library: Masterfile p.5, Jean Marc Blache p.21; White Scar Caves: p.26.

Cover photograph reproduced with permission of Oxford Scientific Films/Michael Pitts.

Our thanks to Sue Graves and Hilda Reed for their advice and expertise in the preparation of this book.

Every effort has been made to contact copyright holders of any material reproduced in this book. Any omissions will be rectified in subsequent printings if notice is given to the publishers.

Contents

Any words appearing in the text in bold, **like this**, are explained in the Glossary.

What is a cave?

A cave is a place where rock has worn away to leave a hollow space under the ground or in a hillside.

rock

hollow space

This cave has been made under the ground.

It takes thousands of years for a cave to form

hollow
space

The deepest
cave in the
world is in
France. It is
about 1602
metres deep!

rock

This cave has been made under the sea.

There are caves all over the world. They are found along the coast, under the ground and in the sides of mountains and hills. Some caves are very deep.

Making sea caves

The sea is very powerful. All along the coast, strong waves batter the cliffs. Over many years the sea wears away the rock.

foot of the cliff

waves

Every day, the sea crashes against the foot of the cliff and wears away the rock.

cliff

The sea has started to make a hole at the foot of this cliff.

hole

The sea eats into the bottom of the cliff. If there is a weak part in the rock, the sea can start to make a hole in the bottom of the cliff.

How sea caves grow

crack

cliffs

cave

The cracks in these cliffs have become bigger. The cracks become caves.

In some places, the bottom of a cliff begins to crack. The cracks are made bigger and bigger by the sea until they become caves.

Smugglers used to hide stolen treasure in caves.

8

blow-hole

Sea-water shoots up through a blow-hole in the roof of a cave.

Some sea caves have cracks in the roof. The sea crashes against the cracks. In time, this makes a hole called a **blow-hole**.

Making an arch

Two sea caves sometimes meet back-to-back, as the rock between them is worn away. This makes an **arch** in the rock.

arch

An arch is made when two caves meet.

Off the coast of the Isle of Wight in the UK, there are some famous stacks called the Needles.

stacks

These pillars of rock are on the coast of Australia.

Over many years, the roof of the arch is worn away. It falls down into the sea. This leaves a pillar of rock standing up in the sea. This is called a **stack**.

Underground caves

Caves are sometimes found underground. They are almost always found in places where the rock is made of **limestone**.

limestone hills

These limestone hills have caves under them.

Prehistoric people lived in caves, usually near the entrance where it was warmer and lighter.

Rain trickles down through the limestone to the rocks below.

Limestone is **dissolved** by rainwater. The water trickles down through cracks in the ground, and slowly wears away the rocks below. Eventually a cave is made.

13

The cave grows

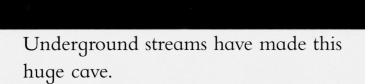

cave roof

tunnel

Underground streams have made this huge cave.

Over thousands of years, underground streams **dissolve** the **limestone**. Cracks in the rock grow bigger and bigger until they make huge tunnels and caves.

boat

This underground cave
is flooded.

water

Some underground caves and tunnels are flooded
with water. Others are dry.

People can only visit some caves in a boat.

In the cave

Look at the strange rock shapes that have grown in this cave.

limestone

The drops of water that trickle underground contain tiny pieces of **limestone**. Some of the drops dry up as they fall, and leave the tiny rock pieces behind. These pile up inside caves.

Fingers of rock hang from the roof of a cave. They are called **stalactites**. Pillars of rock grow up from the floor of a cave. They are called **stalagmites**.

stalactites

stalagmites

Stalactites and **stalagmites** grow very slowly over thousands of years.

The longest stalactites have been found in Brazil. They are about 10 metres long. The tallest stalagmite is in a cave in Slovakia. It measures 32 metres.

17

Hill caves

cave drawings

People made these drawings in this cave in Algeria thousands of years ago.

Caves are made in mountains and hills by the wind, wet weather and running water. They have been used for shelter for thousands of years.

Cave paintings, such as the one in this picture, often show the sorts of animals that people hunted long ago.

In some places, shepherds still use caves to shelter their sheep. Many wild animals, such as bats, use caves for shelter, too.

bats

Bats rest in caves by day and go out to feed at night.

Lots of animals such as bats, birds, fish, insects and even snakes like to live in caves.

Exploring caves

People who study caves are called **speleologists**.
They study the rocks and draw maps of the
tunnels and caves.

stalactites

tunnel

stalagmite

These speleologists are studying an
underground tunnel.

speleologist

Speleology first began in France
in the late nineteenth century.

These men are wearing **protective** clothing in this flooded tunnel.

torch

protective clothing

Exploring caves can be dangerous because they are sometimes flooded when it rains. To be safe, speleologists often take diving gear and boats.

Cave map 1

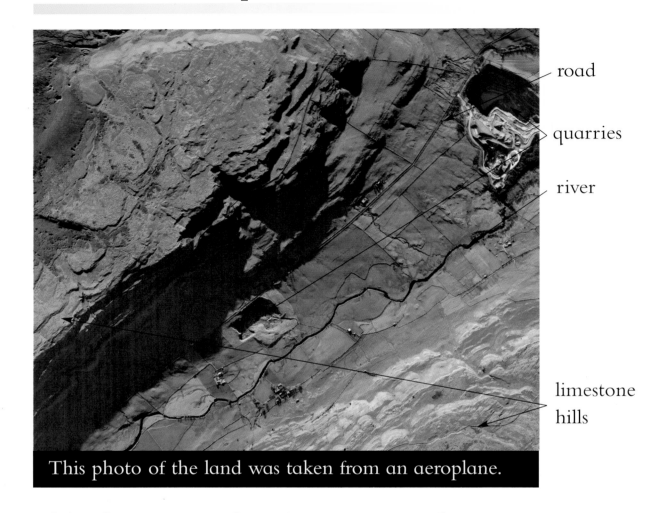

road

quarries

river

limestone hills

This photo of the land was taken from an aeroplane.

This photo was taken from an aeroplane. You can see high **limestone** hills. Between the hills, you can see a river and a road. You can also see two **quarries** by the road.

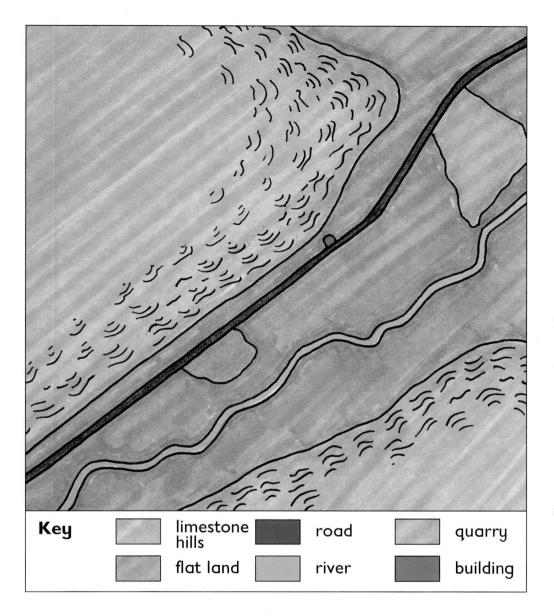

Key

▨	limestone hills	▧	road	▨	quarry
▨	flat land	▨	river	▨	building

Maps are pictures of the land. This map shows us the same place as the photo. Use the key to find the limestone hills, flat land and the river.

Cave map 2

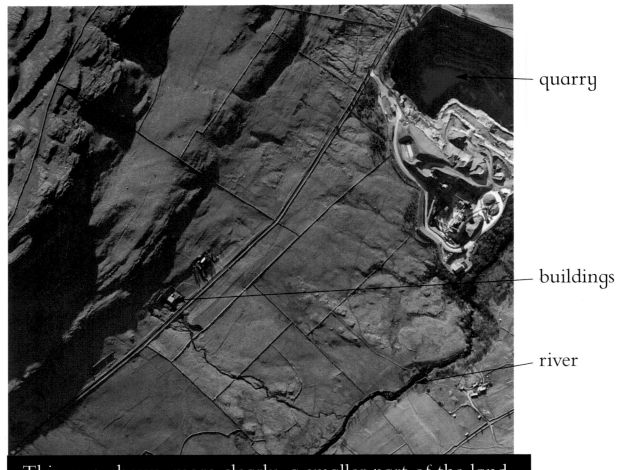

quarry

buildings

river

This map shows, more clearly, a smaller part of the land.

This photo shows a smaller part of the land, but you can see it more clearly. You can see some buildings along the road. One of the buildings is the entrance to caves. The caves are under the hills.

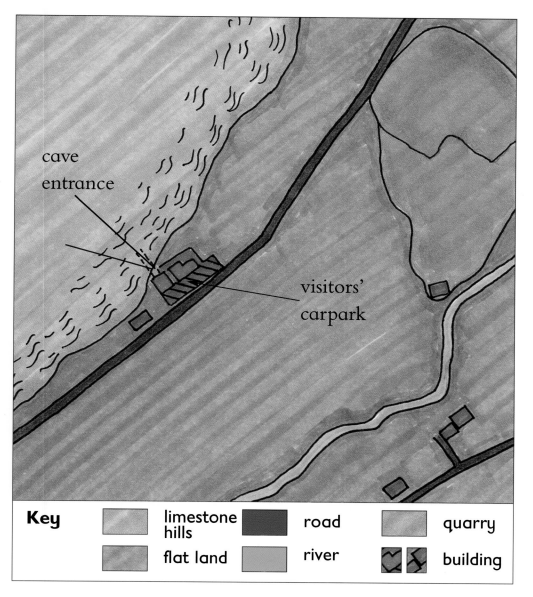

Key

	limestone hills		road		quarry
	flat land		river		building

Maps give people useful information. This map shows how to get to the caves. Find the buildings at the entrance of the cave. What is the black striped area at the back of them?

Cave map 3

stalactites

visitors

This is a photo of Battlefield Cavern.

One of the underground caves is called
Battlefield Cavern. It has many **stalactites**.
People reach it by an underground tunnel.

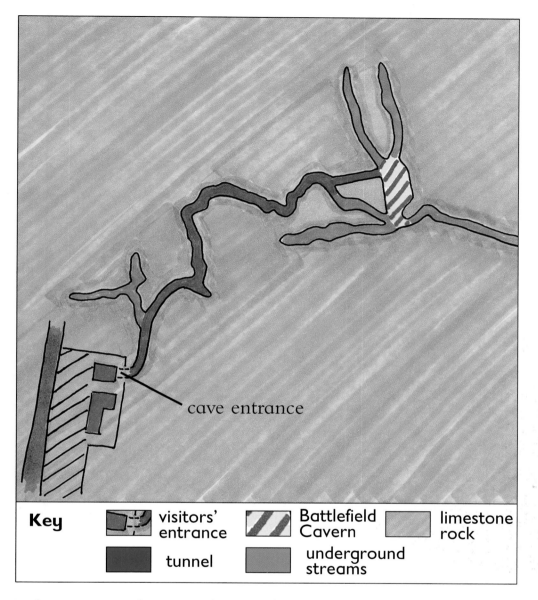

cave entrance

Key

visitors' entrance	Battlefield Cavern	limestone rock	
tunnel	underground streams		

This map shows the way from the cave entrance to Battlefield Cavern through an underground tunnel. It also shows some underground streams.

Amazing cave facts

- The world's largest cave is on the island of Borneo, Australasia. It is called the Sarawak Chamber.

- It would have room for 800 tennis courts inside it!

A photo of Sarawak Chamber, the largest cave in the world.

- The biggest cave system in the world is in Kentucky, USA. It is called the Mammoth Cave National Park. It has caves that stretch for more than 560 kilometres. That's about the same distance from London to Edinburgh!

Glossary

a
b
c
d
e
f
g
h
i
j
k
l
m
n
o
p
q
r
s
t
u
v
w
x
y
z

arch   curved piece of rock on top of two pillars

blow-hole   hole in the roof of a cave. Sea-water gushes up through the hole.

dissolve   disappear in water, like sugar in tea

limestone   a kind of rock that dissolves in rainwater

protective   something that keeps people or things safe

quarry   place where sand or stone is dug out of the ground

speleologist   person who studies caves

stack   the pillar of rock left standing in the sea when an arch falls down

stalactite   finger of rock that grows down from the roof of a cave

stalagmite   pillar of rock that grows up from the floor of a cave

More books to read

Steven Kramer.

Caves.

Lerner Publishing, 1995

Donald M. Silver and Patricia J. Wynne.

One Small Square: Cave.

Learning Triangle Press, 1997

Index

Titles in the *What are ...?* series include:

Hardback   0 431 02440 5

Hardback   0 431 02442 1

Hardback   0 431 02441 3

Hardback   0 431 02439 1

Find out about the other titles in this series on our website www.heinemann.co.uk/library